NATIONAL GEOGRAPHIC

Ladders

Mixed-Up Matter

GENRE Humorous Fiction **Read to find out** what happens when Milo mixes matter.

Milo, Simon, and the BARKING GLOOP

by Allan Woodrow
illustrated by Aaron Blecha

Standing in his bedroom science lab, Milo adjusted his Durasee 3000 super-safe, fog-resistant safety goggles. These high-tech goggles protected against everything from laser beams to battery acid. When it came to lab equipment, Milo spared no expense. After all, lab safety was important to scientists, and Milo was a kid scientist through and through. He even had a plaque on his wall: *World's Smartest 10-Year-Old Scientist.* His mother had made it for him.

Milo tied his lab apron and pulled on a pair of thick, oversized rubber safety gloves. "Today," he announced, "we're making history!"

Simon, Milo's best friend and lab partner, peered at the blue blob bubbling in a jar. Simon put on his safety goggles, too, because he liked assisting Milo in lab **experiments.** "That doesn't look like history," Simon joked, poking the jar. "What is it?"

"It's a simple combination of liquid starch and glue. Separately, they are very ordinary, but stirring them together produces a different type of **matter,** called gloop."

Simon eyed Milo suspiciously, recalling how Milo never performed easy experiments.

"I also added a few secret ingredients, which have caused certain changes in the gloop's physical **properties.** The last ingredient I'm adding is *this*!" Milo held up a small jar, which contained something fuzzy.

"Is that hair?"

"I plucked them from Whiskers, Mr. Farfel's St. Bernard. Ordinary gloop bounces, molds, and stretches, but this matter will also sit up, beg, and do tricks! I call it Silly Puppy!"

"This sounds like a very bad idea."

"Nonsense!" Milo exclaimed. "It's all in the name of science."

Milo stirred the dog hairs into the mixture while Simon looked on nervously. He didn't like this one bit. Milo's experiments often went haywire.

The gloop shuddered, gasped, and almost jumped out of its container. "I think we should stop this," whispered Simon, watching as the mixture started to expand. A few dog hairs sprang out, but then the gloop did nothing.

"Well, I guess that wasn't so bad," said Simon, sighing with relief.

Simon lifted the Silly Puppy out of the jar, stretched it, rolled it into a ball, and bounced it against a wall. He then shaped it into a dog. "I guess I worried for nothing," he said with a nervous laugh.

Milo scratched his head and adjusted his Durasee 3000 super-safe, fog-resistant safety goggles. "I don't understand. According to my calculations the gloop should be sitting up and begging for our attention."

"Maybe it needs a dog treat," suggested Simon. "Dogs love doing tricks for treats."

"That's a great idea, but I don't have any dog treats," said Milo.

The neighbor's cat meowed. Apparently Fluffball had been watching from the windowsill.

"I'll shoo her away," said Simon, marching to the window.

"No! Stop!" shouted Milo, but he shouted too late. Simon opened the window, the cat meowed, and Silly Puppy barked.

But Silly Puppy did more than bark. It stood up on its four gloopy paws and leapt out the window.

"After it!" yelled Milo.

They dashed down the stairs, out the door, and onto the front lawn. Fluffball crouched on a high tree branch while Silly Puppy yipped and growled below. The cat seemed to be enjoying herself, perched safely in the tree.

Simon reached down to snare Silly Puppy, but the gloop was slippery and slimed out of his hands.

Milo and Simon chased Silly Puppy around the tree. Meanwhile Fluffball crouched on her branch, watching Silly Puppy outrun the boys.

Mr. Farfel walked by with his St. Bernard, Whiskers. They stopped to look—after all, it's not every day you see two boys chasing gloop around a tree.

Whiskers barked excitedly and then bolted forward, his leash slipping out of Mr. Farfel's hands. The dog joined Silly Puppy in growling, barking, and running laps.

Luckily, Mr. Farfel was prepared for such emergencies. He held out a handful of dog treats toward Whiskers, who caught a whiff and quickly gave up the chase.

Simon grabbed some treats from Mr. Farfel, too. Getting Silly Puppy to stop barking took some coaxing, but finally it sniffed the snacks and forgot about Fluffball.

Simon scooped up Silly Puppy, and Fluffball jumped down from her branch. The cat stuck out her tongue at them. Silly Puppy yapped, squirmed, and begged to be let down, but Simon held it tightly. "It's awfully jumpy for a glob of gloop," he said, a tad tongue-tied and out of breath.

Milo bent over and plucked a few hairs from Fluffball before she could dart out of reach. "These will work perfectly," Milo said. "Let's get back to my bedroom lab. I have an idea that I think we should try."

Back inside its container, the gloop seethed and bubbled. Simon took a long, deep breath, now that everything was under control again.

"Adding dog hairs was a mistake," said Milo. "Dogs are too easily excited, whereas cats are much calmer." Milo held up Fluffball's cat hairs and dropped them into the mixture. "This new matter will have some of the properties of a cat. We can call it Silly Purry."

Simon shook his head. He thought this idea sounded even worse than the first one.

"The process will take a few minutes to finish. Let's grab a snack downstairs," said Milo. "Science always makes me hungry."

Simon followed Milo out the door, taking one last worried look at the bubbling mixture behind them.

As he closed the door, he didn't notice the mouse scampering on the desk. Nor did he see the gloop oozing over the container, licking its silly-purry lips.

Check In What caused the gloop to act first like a dog, then like a cat?

GENRE How-To Article

Read to find out how to mix matter to make gloop.

HOW TO MAKE GLOOP

by Stacey Klaman
illustrated by Aaron Blecha

You may be wondering, "Is gloop more of a solid or a liquid?" Weirdly, gloop has **properties** that allow it to act like both a solid *and* a liquid. Like a liquid, gloop takes the shape of the container it's left in. It oozes and flows over surfaces, too. Like a solid, gloop can hold its own unique shape. Follow this procedure to make your own gloop!

SAFETY

- Wear an apron, goggles, and gloves when making gloop.
- Wash your hands after handling gloop.
- If you use food coloring, keep the gloop off your clothes.

WHAT YOU NEED

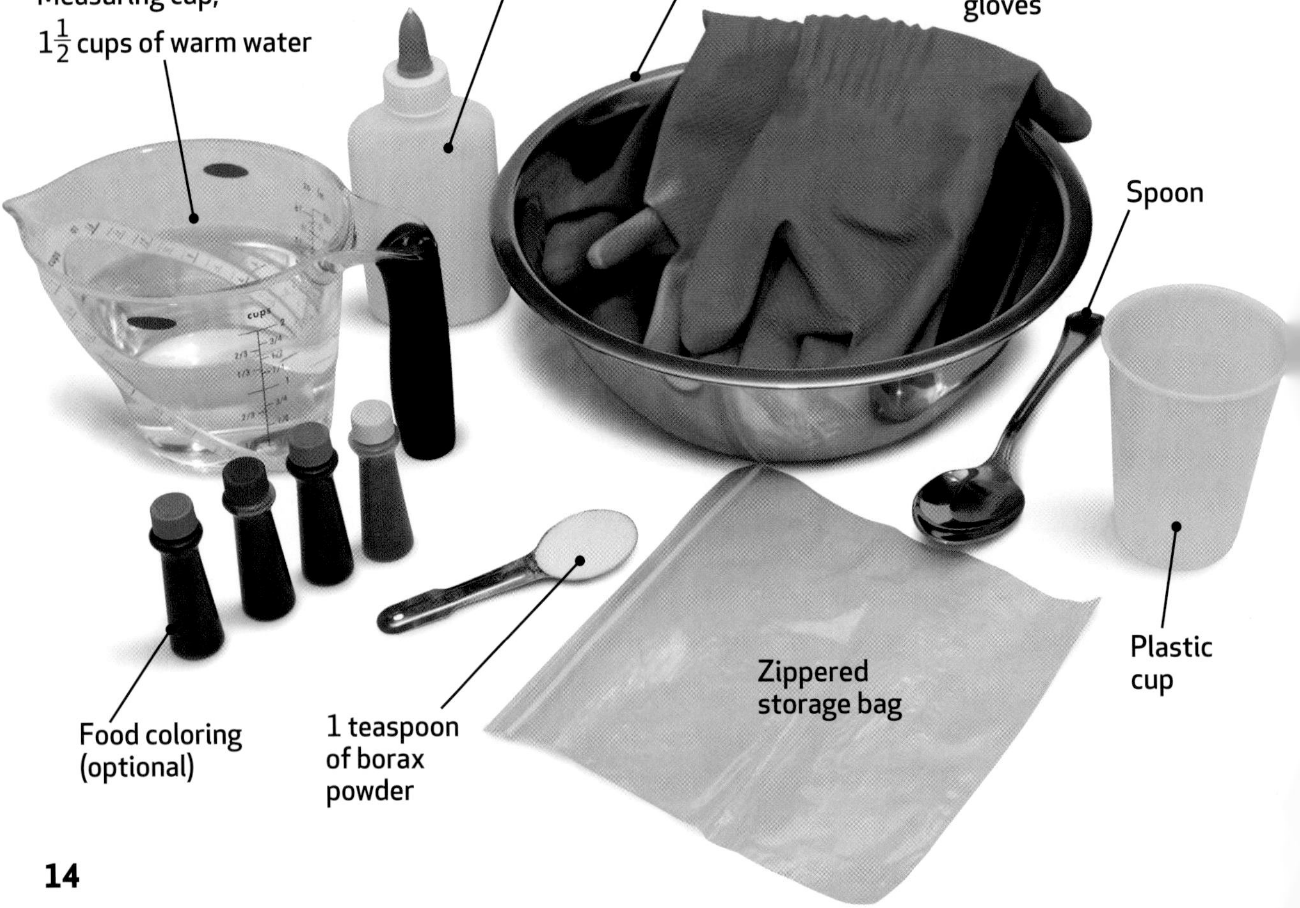

STEP 1

Pour the glue into the mixing bowl. Fill the empty glue bottle with 1 cup of warm water. Put the cap back on. Shake the bottle. Take off the cap and pour the water into the bowl. Stir the mixture with a spoon.

STEP 2

If you don't want your gloop to be white, then try an **experiment** with your favorite color food coloring. You can also use the chart to mix up a color. The numbers show about how many drops to use.

MIXING COLORS

SHADES				
Turquoise	-	-	8	2
Brown	14	8	-	4
Grape	10	-	2	-
Lime	-	6	-	2
Pistachio	-	2	-	8
Orange	4	6	-	-
Peach	2	4	-	-
Salmon	6	4	-	-

STEP 3

In the plastic cup, mix $\frac{1}{2}$ cup of warm water and one teaspoon of borax powder. Stir the **solution.** Dissolve as much of the powder as you can. Then slowly stir the borax solution into the bowl of glue and water.

STEP 4

When your gloop doesn't look or feel like a liquid anymore, pick it up. Knead, or squeeze, the gloop with your hands. Do this until it feels dry. The more you knead your gloop, the less sticky it will be. When you are finished, the gloop should feel firm. It should feel rubbery, not brittle.

Store your gloop in a zippered storage bag in the fridge. This will prevent mold from growing on it.

WHAT HAPPENS?

Separately, the glue and borax solutions are liquids. When you add the borax and water solution to the glue and water solution, a new material forms with a unique set of physical properties. At times this new material seems like a liquid, at other times like a solid. For example, if you place gloop on the back of your hand, it will remain firm like a solid. After a few moments, however, it will lose its shape and begin to ooze over your hand and between your fingers like an extremely thick liquid!

WHAT CAN YOU DO WITH GLOOP?

Try to shape gloop into an animal, bounce it like a ball, stretch it like a rubber band, or tear it like rubber or plastic. You can do a lot with gloop because of its unusual properties.

Check In What are some of the physical properties of gloop?

GENRE Humorous Fiction

Read to find out what happens when Milo builds a model volcano.

Milo, Simon, and the GIANT ERUPTION

by Allan Woodrow
illustrated by Aaron Blecha

Milo, kid scientist through and through, adjusted his Durasee 3000 super-safe, fog-resistant safety goggles, tightened his scruffy lab apron, and took a big whiff. His mother was cooking dinner in the kitchen. Milo was hungry, but he had more important things to do than eat.

"We'll be outside doing **experiments,** Mom!" yelled Milo.

"Don't you get into any trouble!" his mother shouted back.

"Who, me?" asked Milo innocently. Simon, Milo's best friend and lab assistant, shook his head. Milo's science experiments always caused trouble.

"Today, I've built a small pretend volcano," said Milo. "When you **combine** baking soda with vinegar and a little dish detergent, a gas is produced, pressure builds, and . . . BAM! Instant **eruption**!"

"Is that how real volcanoes work?" asked Simon.

"It is a little like how a volcano works, but it's different, too. A real volcano spews glowing-hot lava. This lava is perfectly safe and easy."

Simon stared at Milo, waiting to hear the rest of the experiment details. Milo didn't "do" easy. He did difficult and troublesome.

"I also combined with the vinegar mixture some extra ingredients, like a few grasshoppers, kangaroo saliva, jumping beans, and several fleas from Fluffball, the neighbor's cat. Those things all jump, so the lava will erupt higher in the air. I also added red-colored rocket fuel to strengthen this **property.**"

"This sounds like a very bad idea," said Simon, always the voice of reason.

"It's a great idea, and it's all in the name of science!" said Milo.

Milo emptied a box of baking soda into the fake volcano. Then he grabbed the gallon-sized jug of rocket-powered lava and raised it over the opening.

"I think you should just pour a little in first," suggested Simon, taking two steps backward. "Better safe than sorry."

"Good idea," Milo said, tilting the jug and spilling a few drips inside the open mouth. The mixture shot upward ten feet into the air.

"That was awesome!" exclaimed Simon, clapping.

"Imagine the reaction if I dumped the rest of it in!" said Milo, holding up the jug.

Simon shook his head nervously. "Let's pour just a little bit more. Better safe than sorry, remember?"

Milo sighed and splashed a little liquid into the opening.

Almost instantly, a gusher of red shot into the air, up and up and up, splashing the window of an airplane flying thousands of feet above them.

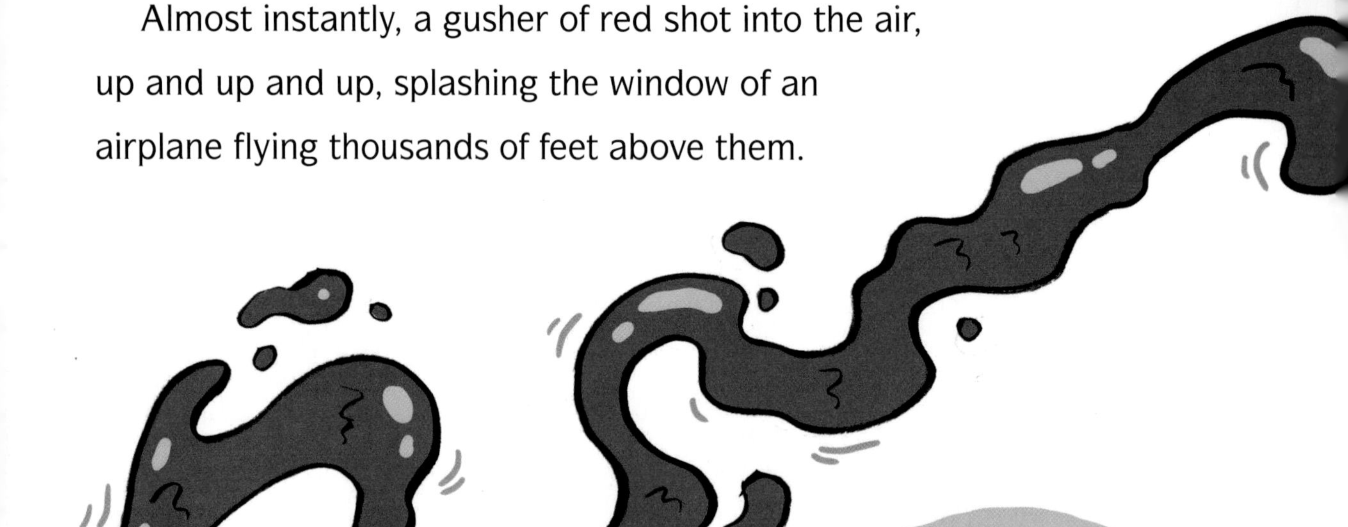

"Now we'll pour it all in," said Milo.

"I don't think we should," warned Simon. "What about our rule, 'better safe than sorry'?"

"What's the worst thing that could happen?" asked Milo. Simon didn't answer, but he could think of lots of possible worst things.

Milo added a fresh box of baking soda, then tipped over the jug, and the bright red liquid gushed inside.

Z Z Z
AIR

Nothing happened. Milo scratched his head, adjusted his high-tech goggles, and tugged on the sleeves of his roomy rubber gloves. He leaned over the volcano to get a better look inside. "I think some of the mixture's properties are changing because I can see the rocket-powered lava bubbling. So why is there no eruption?"

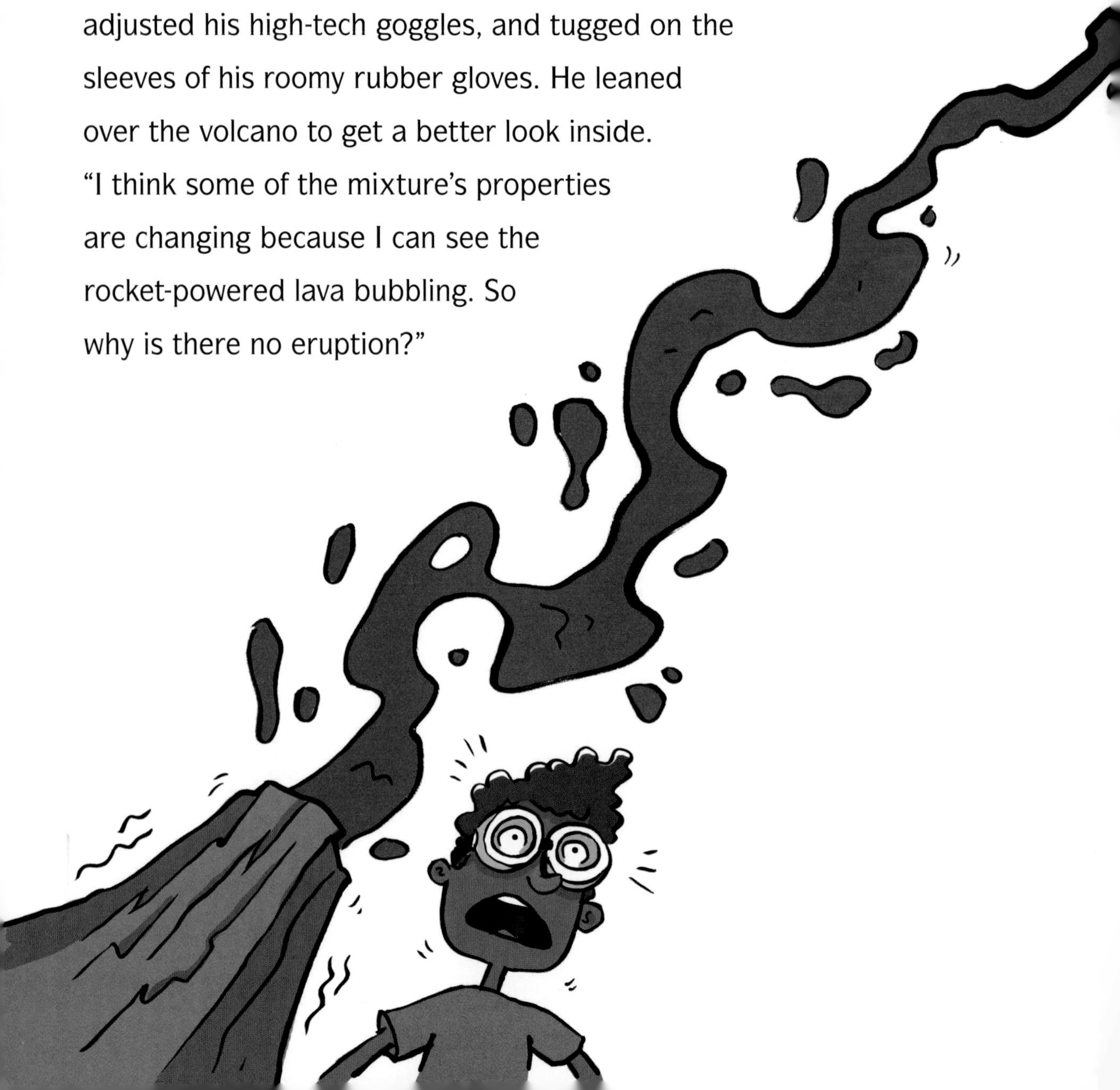

With a surprise explosion loud enough to be heard three blocks away, the super-powered lava mixture rocketed up into the sky, taking Milo with it.

Milo passed a bird that he recognized was a common wood stork. As a scientist, Milo knew all about animals, too. "What are you doing here?" said Milo. "Your species is usually found closer to water."

The stork didn't answer. Instead it yapped angrily.

But the rocket-powered lava didn't stop climbing. It soared even higher, all the way through the clouds and up into space, where Milo narrowly missed colliding into an astronaut on a spacewalk. The boy scientist hung in space for a moment, smiled, waved, and then started to fall.

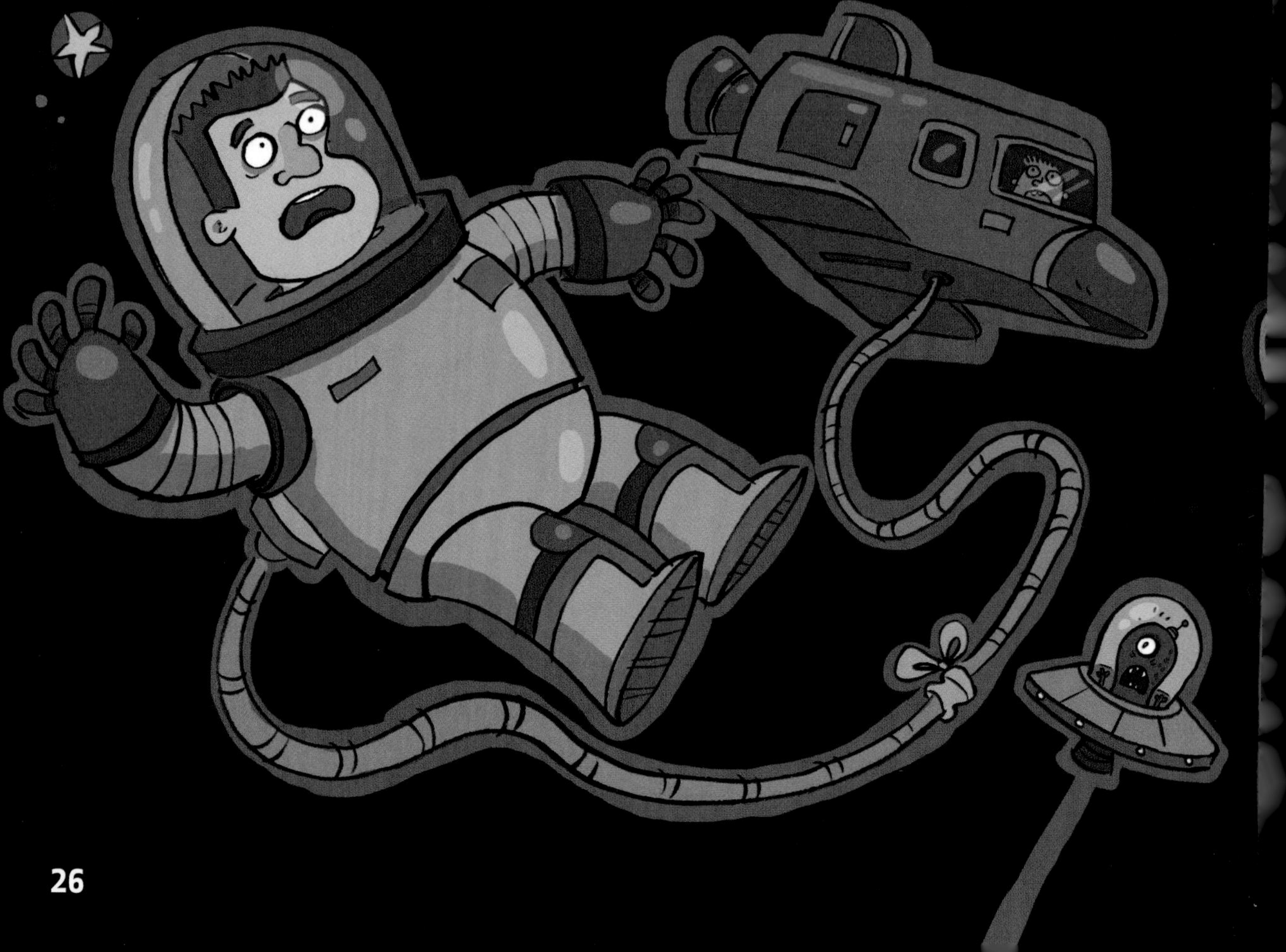

If you've never fallen from space, and it is highly unlikely that you have, you can't appreciate how fast you drop. Milo could compute his speed by taking into account his weight, air pressure, wind, and other factors. But none of that would help him go any slower. He would soon splat on the ground, unless something slowed him down.

Milo passed the same clouds he had seen while he was blasting up, and the same wood stork, too. Milo grabbed the bird's leg, and the stork squawked and beat its wings as fast as it could. It didn't stop Milo's fall, not completely, but it slowed him down. The stork flapped faster and faster, and Milo fell slower and slower, until he landed light as a feather on the ground next to Simon.

Simon closed his mouth, which had been gaping open in astonishment the entire time. "Are you okay?"

"Never better," said Milo, waving goodbye to the stork. "Imagine finding a wood stork this far from water! Do you want a turn going up into space, Simon?"

"No!" said Simon with a vigorous shake of his head. "Besides, there's no more lava mixture left."

"Well . . . maybe there's some left," said Milo.

"Where is it?" asked Simon in surprise, looking around.

"I left it in the kitchen," said Milo.

Inside the house, a delicious-smelling haze filled the kitchen as Milo's mother cooked dinner. There was so much steamy haze, Milo's mother couldn't see very well. She accidentally added some baking soda to the pot instead of salt.

Then she grabbed the spaghetti sauce to pour in. At least she thought it was the spaghetti sauce.

KABOOM!

“I think,” gasped Simon, “your mom found the rocket-powered lava!”

From somewhere deep inside the house, Milo’s mother hollered angrily, “Milo, you’re in big trouble!”

Milo adjusted his high-tech goggles and pulled off his rubber gloves. “All in the name of science,” he gulped.

Check In What caused Milo’s volcano model to erupt?

Discuss Characters, Stories, and Procedures

1. Tell about some of the ways you think the three pieces in this book are linked.

2. Compare and contrast the two stories about Milo and Simon. What mistake did Milo make in both of his experiments? Why did it matter?

3. In "How to Make Gloop," why is it important to follow the steps in order? What do you think might happen if you followed the steps out of order?

4. In what ways are Milo and Simon alike and different? How might the events in the last story have been different if Simon were in charge?

5. What do you still wonder about changing or mixing matter? What would be some good ways to find more information?